GOD IS ALL-GOOD

Brown Bear and Red Goose have two children, a gosling named Charity and a cub named John. They all believe in God.

God Is All-Good
2013

ISBN-13: 978-1483997452
ISBN-10: 1483997456

God Is All-Good

The Attributes of God for Children

One afternoon Charity and John came home from school. It was clear that something was bothering Charity. She decided to talk to Papa about it.

"Papa," she said, "One of the boys at school said that it's not really wrong to cheat. It might be wrong for me, but it's all right for him."

"Well, that depends on where right and wrong come from," Papa replied. "If there were no God, then I think your friend would be right. What we call 'right' and 'wrong' would be just a matter of opinion. In order to live together, people would adopt certain rules about how to act. But there wouldn't be anything really *wrong* about breaking the rules or anything really *good* about obeying them."

"Just think what that means!" Mama said. "If there is no real right and wrong, then there's nothing wrong with hurting innocent children."

"But, Mama," Charity exclaimed, "It's wrong to hurt children!"

"Of course, it is," said Mama, putting her wing around her. "That shows that your friend was mistaken. Some things are *really* right or wrong, regardless of what anyone thinks."

"So then where do right and wrong come from?" asked John.

"Let's see what the Bible says," Papa answered. Opening his Bible, he read, "And the Lord said, 'You shall be holy; for I the Lord your God am holy' (Leviticus 19.1-2).

"What does it mean to be holy?" Papa asked.

"To always do what is right," answered John.

"That's correct," said Papa. "Being holy involves being perfectly good, being without sin. The Bible says that the reason we should be good is because God is perfectly good and wants us to be like Him. Right and wrong come from God. We should do whatever God commands."

Charity thought hard for a minute. Then she said, "But why does God command the things that He does? If He commands them because they're right, then we still don't know where right and wrong come from. And if He just makes up His commands, then He could command anything!"

"You're really thinking hard about this! But those aren't the only two alternatives," explained Papa. "God's very nature is goodness. He is perfect justice, kindness, honesty, love, and so on. His commands flow out of His perfectly good nature. So His commands aren't just made up. But they aren't based on anything outside of God either. His commands are rooted in His own perfect goodness."

"And we should obey His commands," said John.

"That's right," said Papa. "God says we should be holy, just as He is holy. God is all-good, and He is the source of right and wrong for us."

But do we always obey His commands?" Mama asked.

"No," said Charity and John quietly.

"That's why we need a Savior," Mama continued. "We've all broken God's commands and so are guilty before God. We need someone to save us from our sin."

"Jesus!" said John brightly. "He saves us from our sins."

"Right!" said Papa. "And do you know what's wonderful about God's perfect goodness? Even though it's God's perfect goodness which shows us we are sinners, it's also God's perfect goodness which saves us. Everyone who believes in Jesus shares in God's own goodness, which makes us ready to go to heaven."

Papa and Mama snuggled up with Charity and John. "Isn't God good?" they exclaimed.

Memory verse:
"And the Lord said, 'You shall
be holy; for I the Lord your God
am holy'." – Leviticus 19:1-2

Books in the "What is God Like?" series

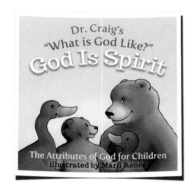

I. God is Spirit

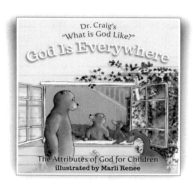

II. God is Everywhere

III. God is Forever

IV. God is Self-Sufficient

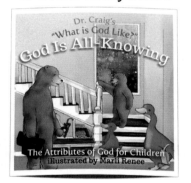

V. God is All-Knowing

VI. God is All-Powerful

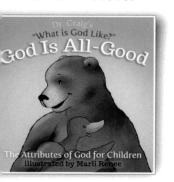

VII. God is All-Good

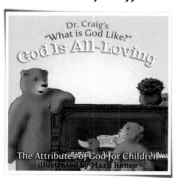

VIII. God is All-Loving

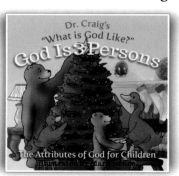

IX. God is Three Persons

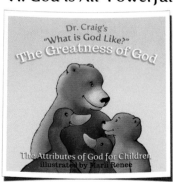

X. The Greatness of God